Who Is Oprah Winfrey?

The Path She Chose to Success

The Story of a Girl Who Was Born Into Poverty and Then Went On to Become the Richest African American Woman of the 20th Century

By Phil Cooper

"Be thankful for what you have; you will end up having more. If you concentrate on what you don't have, you will never, ever have enough."

— Oprah Winfrey

Table of Contents

Introduction

In life, we face countless challenges, and then at one point, these challenges seem never-ending. You struggle repeatedly, but it feels like the reward you get for your efforts is too small. We read stories online and biographies. We watch reality TV shows to stay up to date with what famous people are doing to stay at the stage they have reached today.

Now, we have 12-year-old millionaires, and then there are people like Mark Cuban and Oprah Winfrey. These billionaires live luxurious lives not because they were given the opportunity to test their skills. They chose to put everything on the line and spend every waking moment of their life turning their dream into reality. These people could never even fathom they would enjoy the comforts they have today.

Did you know that reading success stories about professionals stimulates a person's motivational enzyme and pushes them to emulate their path to success?

Whether you aim to get rich or create a name for yourself that money follows you, you need to be willing to give your best despite the odds stacked against you, and that's what Oprah Winfrey did.

Today, we all know her as the multi-award-winning TV host and philanthropist known for bringing out the truth and giving advice that hits close to home. Who can forget her famous interview with the former Duke and Duchess of Sussex – *Harry and Meghan Markel* that sensationalized Britain, *Kim Kardashian* on her sex tape and her 72-day marriage to Kris

Humphries, *Rihanna* on her abusive relationship with Chris Brown, *Michael Jackson* on his surgery, and *Ellen DeGeneres* when she came out and talked for the first time about being openly gay for the first time.

There are dozens of other famous names who were never fans of speaking publicly and being under the spotlight but opened up to Oprah. One could say that she has a way of making people step out of their comfort zone and unburden their hearts and minds to someone they know will understand.

Oprah crossed one obstacle after another to achieve what she had set out for. Enduring the hardest situations that life threw at her, she became a stronger and bigger person. Even in her mistake, she sought lessons to be learned, which helped her accomplish a lot.

No one says this, but for Oprah, the hardworking person she is today is thanks to what she went through. It's been said that for the universe to show you the right path, you need to fall multiple times but not give up. You have to have the energy and patience to stand back up *as* many times you fall.

Yes, Oprah is a billionaire, but no one handed her the fortune she holds today. Our world is divided by color, and this was also the case back then. Being a black woman made things harder for Oprah, but she never let anything, or anyone hurt her pride and who she is. She overcame every obstacle and persevered.

From looking closely at Oprah's personality traits, we learn that every person should take responsibility for what they do in their lives and push themselves to improve those around them and the world.

Oprah didn't have the kind of regal or flashy upbringing like the famous people she interviewed. She was raised in the small city of Kosciusko, Mississippi, by her grandmother. Her childhood was modest. However, her humble background never diminished her ambitions. Oprah became a trailblazer in the entertainment industry with her natural candor and easy-going attitude. To this day, she is the most notable television personality.

The Story of Oprah Winfrey

"Always continue the climb. It is possible for you to do whatever you choose if you first get to know who you are and are willing to work with a power that is greater than ourselves to do it."

Oprah had and still has the kind of career which seems impossible for any woman to achieve or handle. Yet, she does it beautifully. Surprisingly, she encourages other women to not follow in her footsteps but create their own to set a standard for their children.

The accomplished media mogul and actress has smashed through barriers and defied many odds to achieve the position she is in today. You might not know that Oprah battled adversity her entire life.

Born on January 29, 1954, in Kosciusko, Mississippi, Oprah Gail Winfrey lived a troubled childhood. Her father, Vernon Winfrey, and mother, Vernita Lee, weren't a couple. They lived separate lives, and Oprah wasn't a part of them. Her grandmother Hattie Mae Lee raised her because her mother moved up north for work. They lived in extreme poverty, and conditions were so dire that Oprah wore clothes made from potato sacks.

Oprah's early years were occupied with learning. Her grandmother took her to church and taught her how to read. She would stand up in Sunday sermons and read passages aloud. Being born into poverty didn't erase Oprah's desire to learn. She was a gifted child, and her passion for speaking increased over the years. She even envisioned a future in it.

Her grandmother wanted Oprah's dream to come true. So, she did everything in her power to teach her how to read and write. By the age of 3, Oprah could read Bible verses and even recite them fluently. Astonished by how well Oprah read, the people who visited church frequently named her "The Preacher."

It was during this time her passion for speaking took shape. She would often interview the birds around her and the dolls in her room, imagining she was on stage and the animals were the audience. Years later, reflecting on her speaking confidence, Oprah realized that it was her grandmother from whom she got the encouragement to speak in front of a crowd.

At 5, she started kindergarten but moved to the 1st grade because the teachers saw her talented she was. These were the years when Oprah was truly happy as a child.

Soon, she began moving around a lot, and that's when her life changed.

Her grandmother got sick a year later, and Oprah was sent to live with her half-sister and mother in Milwaukee. It is not known whether Oprah got along with her mother and new sister. However, when Oprah turned 7, she was sent to live with her stepmother and father in Nashville a year later.

After a few weeks of adjusting to the change, she settled in nicely and skipped another grade, making it to the 3rd grade. She soon joined the church and got involved in the activities, showing how proficient she was with public speaking.

That summer, she went back to her mom and decided she would stay with her and her two siblings. Unfortunately, at age 9, she experienced sexual abuse. After coming from school, she would babysit her younger siblings as her mother went to work. One fine evening, her 19-year-old cousin came over. Knowing there were no adults present in the house, he raped her.

Things just went downhill from there. As time passed, her uncle and a family friend joined the list of sexual abusers. Oprah discovered she was pregnant and didn't know who the father was at such a young age because she had been raped multiple times. From the ages of 9 to 13, Oprah faced constant abuse.

The abuse was traumatizing, and Oprah didn't know how or whom to talk about it, so she kept it all to herself. It didn't help that her cousin threatened her with pain and death if she revealed what was happening.

With no outlet, Oprah started acting out. She stole, skipped school, and ran away from home. Her mother couldn't handle her tantrum. Not knowing what was happening to her, she forced Oprah to move back to Nashville with her father.

Oprah suffered many emotional and physical effects from what she went through. Nevertheless, she never gave up and kept fighting. She ran away from the house numerous times to escape her problems, but the locals or her father would always find her. Unfortunately, when she turned 14, she received the horrifying news that she was pregnant.

With the father unknown, she decided not to reveal her condition to her family members. For seven months, she hid the secret, but her swollen ankles and body gave away the truth. The day it was all revealed, she went into labor. Unfortunately, her baby couldn't handle the stress and died two weeks later in the hospital. Although what happened was devastating, Oprah held her head high and moved on.

She didn't know that a family member of hers would exploit this information. In 1990, the news about her pregnancy spread like wildfire when it was sold as a sordid story to the tabloid for $19,000. This opened the can worms she had tightly shut to keep her past at bay. However, Oprah says that getting her secret revealed allowed her to let go of the shame and hurt she had been holding on to for years.

In 2015, she showed a new side to the public when she shared her baby's name. During an interview in Australia, a reporter told her that she would get closure and peace if she named her baby. Oprah had given birth to a boy, information she revealed along with the name: Canaan.

"I named him Canaan because Canaan means new land, new life."

Life After Losing a Child

Losing a child breaks many people, but Oprah was stronger than she looked. All she wanted to do was move past the trauma and leave all the pain behind.

However, thoughts about her unborn child kept circulating in her head, and she became suicidal. However, she never did something to harm herself. After being sent to live with her new parents, Oprah began a new life. She started trusting her instincts, which gave her the courage to step foot into the public eye.

Her life took a turn for the better but only because she had willed it so. She took part in beauty pageants, and despite having no sense of fashion or beautification, she won Miss Black Tennessee in 1972 at the age of 17.

After having her moment in the limelight, she knew what she was meant to do. She graced the stage of beauty pageants multiple times, and after being declared the beauty queen, she made the big leap to national television.

At 19, Oprah was hired as a news anchor in Nashville and created history by being the first-ever African American female to do so. She grabbed this golden opportunity eagerly and left Tennessee State University to pursue her dream.

She quickly became a sensation all around the world, and her sparkling personality caught the attention of several news executives.

Things were starting to look up for her. She had a lot more to achieve, and she did.

The Beginning of Her Morning Show Career

Oprah's professional life picked up speed in 1976 when she moved to Baltimore. At first, she resumed her work as a news anchor. Sharp at 6 P.M., she would come on WJZ alongside her newscast Jerry Turner. Though it was her dream to speak in front of such a huge audience, she hadn't prepared for the likes of Turner.

At 22-years-old, she was earning $22,000, which was a great amount for a young person at that time. However, her inexperience was what Turner didn't like.

Turner wanted to be a solo news anchor. Though Turner had agreed to have a co-host, he didn't want an eager and young partner. He would constantly embarrass Oprah on and off-screen.

He would make fun of her education and where she went to school and belittled her at every chance he got.

Oprah was a deeply empathetic person. She cared a lot about people. However, as a reporter, it was her job to mask her emotions while reporting tragic accidents. This became quite difficult for her, and even though she was earning well, the setback felt like she wasn't cut out for this job.

Since Oprah had a caring nature, she could not be unsympathetic to the suffering and woes of people. After reporting some of the accidents, particularly the ones about fire, she would give blankets to the victims. One time, while reporting a funeral, she couldn't bring herself to ask the grieving parents of a dead child about how they felt because she understood the pain of losing a child all too well.

When word about Oprah's behavior reached her boss, she was deemed unfit for reporting. They wanted someone ruthless who would stick to the facts.

Oprah's boss wanted to fire her. However, since she was on contract for one year, she got demoted.

Oprah was transferred to morning TV, where she signed as a co-host on the talk show "People Are Talking." It turns out that this was the break she needed to shine.

The First Talk Show

Oprah's first thought was that getting the anchor position on the talk show after getting demoted would destroy her career. She had worked hard to build an image in front of her audience, and if the talk show wasn't a hit, no one would hire her anymore.

She begged the channel's General Manager to let her go. Instead, the General Manager told her that if the talk show became a success, she would leave a much bigger mark on the community than a news anchor.

And so, in 1978, Oprah hosted the first episode of People Are Talking.

Once again, Oprah's personality and ability to speak her mind brought her unimaginable fame. She and Richard Sher, her co-anchor, interviewed people from different backgrounds and dove deep into their problems.

Her first guest was a character from the American Soap Opera and an ice cream man. When the interview began, Oprah felt this connection with the person, and it dawned on her that she was finally in the right place.

She embraced her role as the talk show host and asked questions that would prompt people to reveal more about them. To make the person feel at ease, she even revealed her secrets, which is something the female audience loved. As a result, the talk show became a raging success and continued with her as the host for seven years.

Though the show had been going well, Oprah received an offer from the American Broadcasting Company for their talk show. They wanted Oprah to work her magic on their failing talk show and bring up its ratings.

The talk show's content didn't hold any appeal, so an episode only lasted half an hour. Talk in the show was mostly focused on traditional issues that women faced.

Oprah didn't like the direction the show was heading in and decided to change the theme to current controversial topics. Within a few months, the talk show became America's highest-rated show. Its popularity rose to such heights that it even surpassed the talk show hosted by Phil Donahue, one of the best talk shows in Chicago at the time.

People commented that Oprah's style did not match Donahue's since his style was more journalism-based, but she made up for it with her empathy.

Oprah's empathy was her main power, which allowed her to coax guests into revealing their problems, which made her talk show a hit.

As the ratings went up, so did the show's run time, which was extended to 1 hour. After a while, Oprah became a brand. The show was named the Oprah Winfrey Show, which was different from regular talk shows.

The show's content kept transforming and mostly addressed views of celebrities, social issues, and more. The show ran from 1986 to 2011 for 25 years and won 47 Daytime Emmy awards.

Success was knocking at Oprah's door in spades. She received an offer from Steven Spielberg and was cast in the movie *The Color Purple*, which was released in December 1985.

By now, Oprah was earning thousands of dollars for a single episode of her talk show. However, since she desperately wanted to be a part of the movie, she took a smaller paycheck. She acted in a few more films and then focused all her attention on her talk show.

The Start of Something New

After the success of her talk show, Oprah decided to open a production company. In 1986, Harpo Productions, Inc. was formed, and 2 years later, it bought the right to the Oprah Winfrey Show.

And that's how Oprah became the first woman to produce her own talk show.

Oprah's business interests extend well beyond Harpo Productions, Inc. She is a partner of a cable channel called Oxygen Media, Inc. and has her hands in many other lucrative deals.

Her success also gave her the title of the most generous philanthropist in the world. In 2000, the Angel Network by Oprah began a "Use Your Life Award" worth $100,000 for people who improved the lives of others through their lives.

She has two successful magazines to her name called O at Home and O, The Oprah Magazine. In 2003, Forbes published the list of top billionaires in America and revealed that Oprah was the first African-American female to land a position on it.

Weight Loss

Oprah has openly talked about how she has struggled with her weight her entire life. In 1988, she told the audience on her talk show how she had lost 67 pounds.

However, a few years later, she had gained the weight back. She instructed her chefs to take control of her diet and was able to lose 90 pounds. Her success allowed her chefs to publish best-selling books on weight loss.

In 2015, Oprah was still trying to maintain her weight. For inspiration, she bought a 10% stake in the company Weight Watchers (WW). She became the company's advisor and got a seat on the board. She would appear in TV ads that helped raise the company's image, which was previously down.

In 2017, Winfrey credited WW for her weight loss journey and revealed that she had been diagnosed with pre-diabetes but had her sugar level under control.

O Magazine and Oxygen Media

In 1999, Oprah debuted Oxygen Media. The company produced online programming and cable for women. This ensured Oprah a spot in the media industry as an influential person. In 2000, the O Magazine was launched, which also became a success.

Oprah Winfrey Network (OWN)

In 2011, the Oprah Winfrey Show ended, and Oprah decided to create her own network, which had a partnership with Discovery Communications.

The network had a rocky start in terms of finances. However, this changed when, at the start of 2013, OWN made headlines when it broadcasted Oprah's exclusive interview with the American Cyclist Lance Armstrong. At that time, the controversy surrounding Lance was a hot topic, and Oprah wanted to show people his side of the story.

Partnership With Apple

Oprah has always been a strong supporter of women. In 2018, Apple offered Oprah a multi-year deal, which allowed her to produce original content for the brand.

In 2019, Oprah announced her Book Club was coming back to Apple TV+ with Ta-Nehisi Coates' The Water Dancer. She also agreed to work as an executive producer on the documentary On the Record. However, she pulled out before it aired in 2020 because of the sexual allegations made against music industry entrepreneur Russell Simmons, who happened to be the documentary's music producer.

The Oprah Winfrey Show has aired in 140 countries. Some of her regular guests, Dr. Mehmet Oz and Dr. Phil McGraw, started their TV shows, which Harpo Productions still produces.

Her generosity is legendary. At the start of her show's 20th season, she gave every member in the studio a Pontiac automobile. As of 2022, Oprah's current net worth is $2.6 billion. Most of her wealth is because of her quick thinking. She invested the money she made from her movies, her production house is worth $65 million, and her current partnership with Apple is worth $1 billion.

Charity, Wealth, and Awards

Oprah believes that every person has a little bit of good in them. Keeping this in mind, she influenced several people with her nature, affable talks, warmth, and kind philosophies, which healed them.

Oprah still is one of the most prominent philanthropists in the United States. She has given around $400 million in the name of education and donated $12 million to the National Museum of African American History and Culture.

Her warmth doesn't just extend to those in need. She treated and still treats her staff very well. In 2006, she rewarded her staff and their families, around a thousand people, with a fully-paid vacation to Hawaii.

Oprah is a strong advocate of LGBT rights and supports gun control. In 2018, when a student ran a campaign on gun control, she donated $500,000 to the cause.

According to Forbes, Oprah was crowned as the world's richest African American woman of the 20th century for three years running. Life Magazine called her the most influential person of the generation.

In 2002, Oprah became the first-ever recipient of the Bob Hope Humanitarian Award by the Academy of Television Arts & Sciences.

In 2005, Oprah was named America's greatest Black Philanthropist in history by Business Week.

With so much fame, Oprah was able to raise millions of dollars for numerous charities. Having faced abuse in the past, she knew what it was like to be poor, wishing for the smallest of happiness.

Oprah's Angel Network, the charity she formed in 1988, has raised more than $50 million for different charitable programs, such as relief to Hurricane Katrina victims and education for girls in South Africa.

She is also a children's rights activist. In 1994, Oprah proposed a bill for it passed by President Bill Clinton and helped create a national database that documents convicted child abusers.

Due to her many contributions, Oprah received the Presidential Medal of Freedom, the highest civilian order, in 2013. It was awarded by Barack Obama, the first African American President of the United States.

In 2018, Marjory Stoneman Douglas High School experienced a tragic shooting, leaving 17 students dead. Oprah announced that she would donate $500,000 to the cause.

Oprah has encouraged children to be curious and pursue education, women to leave their abusive husbands, speak freely about equality, etc. She has touched the lives of millions of people.

In her podcast, Oprah talked about how many people have come up to her and said "Thank you" for something they got to know about on her show. Her connection with her audience is so deep that she still inspires people even after a decade of her show ending. Oprah has passed many hurdles in her life, and today, she stands strong and a proud woman. Though she has been involved in many controversies, none of them took flight because of the career she has created and succeeded in.

Like every celebrity, Oprah, too, has a couple of pet peeves. She doesn't like chewing gum. In fact, she hates when people around her chew gum. She also has a phobia of balloons.

Did you know that her production company, Harpo, is "Oprah" spelled backward? Oprah was great friends with poet and activist Maya Angelou and considered her a friend, sister, and mother-like figure.

The Oprah Winfrey Show changed American culture in many ways. Oprah has given birth to a generation of viewers and has affected millions. Her legacy is the change every person on earth brought to their lives after watching her show or listening to her.

The Secrets Behind Oprah Winfrey's Success

It was in 1976 when Oprah's career began. She started out as a local news reporter and was sent to different Baltimore neighborhoods to interview people. While the task was small, Oprah saw it as an opportunity to gain popularity.

The interviews allowed her to introduce herself to people, which was a good public relations strategy for her. However, she soon lost her position and was demoted to doing weekend features. Her career faced a slump there because now she was reporting about silly things, such as a birthday party for a cockatoo at a local zoo. Oprah still stuck to news reporting because, at least, she was still appearing on TV.

Her career took a turn for the better when she started doing the talk show *People Are Talking*. She felt as if her career would end, but fate had other plans for her. A few years later, she started her talk show, The Oprah Winfrey Show, where she met people from all walks of life and learned a lot.

Her business acumen also allowed her to become a very successful woman. Today, Oprah's knowledge is like an antique treasure box. A peek into it will help you discover the secrets to getting successful and building a life for yourself.

Now that you know about Oprah's history and the challenges she faced in life, you will be able to understand her advice better and take on success.

Rather Than Looking at the Big Picture, Focus on What Comes Next

"You can have it all. Just not at once."

You might feel intimidated by the responsibility you have on your plate. It's alright to take a step back and think about your next move, then the next, and so on. Be careful and thoughtful about your plans and take baby steps. The big picture is still going to stay there. Your perspective will improve it.

Making some missteps is part of every journey. These missteps do not define what you choose to do and how you proceed. Every step matters because it teaches you something new. Eventually, those small steps will become a giant leap, and you will achieve success.

Grab Every Opportunity That Comes Your Way

"I don't believe in failure. Failure is just information and an opportunity to change your course."

Success is not luck! Oprah doesn't believe that luck has anything to do with how a person's life turns out to be. She insists that there are blessings and grace, but grabbing the right opportunity at the right time matters.

Having this belief doesn't mean that you discard luck. If you stop and think about it, luck strikes when a person meets an opportunity head-on with preparation. If you are not prepared, luck won't be in your favor.

Take Risks

"I believe that one of life's greatest risks is never daring to risk."

It's time to let go of your comfort zone. We know that most people are afraid of taking risks. Well, that in itself is the biggest risk. For example, a client just approached you with a huge project. It's a little out of your scope, but if you hire a new team or consult with your old one about their hidden talents, there's a possibility that you might be able to complete it. However, after thoroughly searching the project, you feel it's a huge risk and might jeopardize your reputation in the industry.

Why always go negative? You might also succeed and enter a niche you never thought your business would enter. Yes, you might fail, but as the old saying goes, "You learn from your mistakes."

Start by just saying, "I will take more risks." When the time comes to implement, you might falter. So, prepare yourself mentally first before taking a physical step.

Think Positive

"I know for sure that what we dwell on is who we become."

This advice should be given to people from a young age. We often dwell on the negative, and they influence our future thoughts. Imagine constantly focusing on all the bad things in your life. You beat yourself up for not choosing the second path, for not saying something different, and if you had only...

Such thoughts keep you away from all the good waiting for you beyond regret. Oprah didn't get to where she is today by forgetting what is important in her life. She always moved forward without stepping on anyone's toes. Even when she wrote a suicide note after her family betrayed her, she tore it up and told herself that giving up was not the answer to her problems.

She picked herself up, turned her most painful wounds into wisdom, and remained positive. They say, "You reap what you sow." So, try to sow only good to reap the rewards.

The Sky Is the Limit

"Your true passion should feel like breathing; it's that natural."

You never stop breathing, do you? That's how you should see struggle! You should keep at it until you achieve success, and even after that, don't stop. For example, let's say you have a passion for writing. So, you write a book. It's a huge success, and people love your captivating tale of love. Why stop at one? Now that you know you have a way with words, you can go on and write more books.

The best way to have a clear path to success is to set goals. Success cannot be predicted. It's impossible! However, what you can do is control the journey to it. So, try everything to figure out what works best for you.

Never Stop Improving Yourself

"With every experience, you alone are painting your own canvas, thought by thought, choice by choice."

Your personality makes you who you are. A salesperson has to be friendly and helpful. These aren't qualities they grow up with. They adopt them to be good at what they like.

In the case of Oprah, she loved standing in front of an audience and speaking. She couldn't help being sympathetic, which got her fired from her job.

However, she didn't give up. She kept her style and stayed true to her personality. Her entire career is because of her empathetic listening and warm nature.

Staying true to yourself doesn't mean you don't pursue your passion. You can always gain new qualities, and that's how you improve yourself. Others might point out that working on yourself seems a bit self-centered, but you should ignore them.

Oprah says that you should take such comments as compliments because she believes it takes a strong person to admit there's still room for improvement within them.

You do you!

Believe In Your Dream

"The choice to be excellent begins with aligning your thoughts and words with the intention to require more from yourself."

They say, "Don't dream big, or you will land on your face."

Oprah says, "Have BIG dreams!"

Belief is necessary for achieving success. If you don't believe in yourself, your goals, and your mission, you won't be able to move forward.

Forgive Your Past Mistakes

"Failure is a great teacher. If you're open to it, every mistake has a lesson to offer."

Wisdom is a gift of aging. Who you were ten years ago no longer exists. How often have you come across a memory and thought to yourself, "What was I thinking?"

First, you feel disbelief, which is followed by shame. Finally, you feel disappointed about doing something you would not even think about now.

However, sometimes youthful transgressions are a lesson that teaches you a lot. Back then, you didn't know better, but now you do. Your past mistakes present an amazing opportunity for you to grow and move forward.

Give It Your All and Then Some

"Don't worry about being successful but work toward being significant, and the success will naturally follow."

Control is everything! If you don't trust in your performance, you won't be able to size up or beat the competition. When Oprah started her talk show, she knew the competition that surrounded her. She knew she couldn't control who came on her competitors' shows and didn't on hers. However, she did know that if she gave her best, people would automatically notice her.

Think of working hard as a race. The faster you run, the sooner you reach the finish line. It doesn't matter if you come in 2nd or 3rd. What matters is that you were able to finish what you started.

It took Oprah some time to reach the finish line, but her struggles made her the best talk show host in the world.

Find Your Purpose

"Listen to the rhythm of your own calling, and follow that."

Have you ever thought about your existence? You need to dig a little deeper to find out your purpose on earth. What does this have to do with success?

Here's an example to help you understand the meaning of purpose:

Your New Year's resolution is to lose some weight and get healthy. So, you print out some posters of celebrities that have set realistic fitness expectations and paste them on your wall. Next, you print out a motivational quote, frame it, and hang it right in front of your bed so that every morning when you wake up, it is the first thing you see.

You now have a purpose, and you have dedicated your body and mind to it. If you don't have a purpose yet, stop! Do a little soul searching and focus on what you desire and are passionate about.

Managing Finances – The Towel Theory

Today, Oprah flies in her private jet, owns a couple of million-dollar estates, and spends money on luxurious items that she had never even dreamed of owning as a kid.

There's a secret behind her success, which she has shared openly.

"I still think twice before I buy anything. How will this fit in with what I already have? Am I just caught up in the

This is the philosophy Oprah lives by. It is something she learned from her father. When it comes to financial advice, Oprah is a pro at it. Her book *"Oprah Winfrey: A Rags to Riches Story: How to Overcome Obstacles and Achieve Financial Success"* is full of small tidbits that tell people how to manage their money.

One thing that Oprah is most familiar with is the value of money. She has worked plenty of jobs that paid her a lowly $12,000/year to $100,000/month.

You probably focused on the latter numbers and assumed having this much money would solve all your problems. However, Oprah thinks differently. She believes that when you have a large amount of cash with you, you spend more, bringing debt.

She calls this "The Towel Theory."

According to this theory, Oprah made all her purchases within a limit. Even though she could have splurged on expensive items, such as a car, she stuck to... Towels.

Yes, towels! At first, she bought them from Target and then set her sights on bigger brands such as Saks Fifth Avenue. It was and still is one of her guilty little pleasures.

Oprah says, *"Keep your spending, earning, investing, and saving in balance by living within your means."*

Invest in What You Know

"The truth is I have from the very beginning listened to my instincts. All of my best decisions in life have come because I was attuned to what really felt like the next right move for me."

Stepping out of your comfort zone is a great idea. She has been a strong advocate of Weight Watchers from the time she struggled with her weight.

In 2015, she bought a 10% stake in the company, which cost $6.79/share at the time. By 2018, the price had risen to $100/share.

Oprah believes that investing is all about instincts. If the product holds great value and you believe in it, go all in. Never follow a trend just because people are making money off of it. Start small with $5, and then expand your horizon based on your knowledge.

Diversify Your Income

"There is a flow with your name on it. Your job is to find it and let it carry you to the next level."

You have probably heard the saying, "Nothing stays the same for long." Oprah hit the jackpot when her talk show became successful, and she started making investments. However, she knew that this winning streak wouldn't continue for long, and sooner or later, she would retire. So, she recalculated her success and decided to do a final episode of The Oprah Winfrey Show and then move on.

She then came up with her production house and a magazine. That's how her media empire began. She acted in films, wrote books, and did a lot more within her means.

When diversifying your income, you have to pursue all money-making possibilities but choose the ones you feel you can see through till the end.

Yes, having a 9-to-5 job offers you stability, but sometimes, you need to look around and see what opportunity you can grab based on your skills. Start small with side gigs, and then think big.

Think Before Opening Your Wallet

"The single greatest thing you can do to change your life today would be to start being grateful for what you have right now."

Oprah has won so many awards and trophies that she has a whole wall dedicated to them. Even if she does run out of space, she can always buy another house to display them. However, she doesn't waste her money on frivolous things.

Money in your hand is a blessing, as well as a curse. You can't live without it, but with it, a change ensues within you, which is sometimes not good. Keep in mind luxuries don't affect your conscience. Due to frivolous spending and bad financial decisions, many people with successful careers lost their fortunes. These people include Kim Basinger, 50 Cent, Larry King, and NFL players, such as Andre Rison, Chris McAllister, and Vince Young.

Before spending a dollar on frivolous things, ask yourself: Will this fit into my lifestyle? Is it worth the price? Is buying it necessary? Will it bring me any real satisfaction? Perhaps, I am being wasteful?

You know what you can do to eliminate all these thoughts and make a clear decision – Use a budgeting app to track your spending. It will help you calculate how much is coming in and going out.

For example, if you love eating out, set a dollar amount on it. If you run out before the month ends, refrain from spending even on a cup of coffee you get from the cart outside your office.

Savings, Savings, SAVINGS

"The greatest discovery of all time is that a person can change their future by merely changing their attitude."

Money changes your attitude. Period.

Most people assume that they don't need to plan for the future if they are rich. Take a look at any successful personality, and you will find out that they have made it so far because they made sound financial decisions.

Read any blog post on financial tips, and you are bound to come across the words: *Set a small fortune aside for rainy days*. This approach is great for building a safety net to fall back on.

Money comes and goes. Its fickle personality makes us happy one minute and sad the other. In an interview, Oprah revealed that she has set aside around $50 million in cash for the future. With the way her investments have been appreciating over the years, she probably has added more to it.

You also need an emergency fund; of course, your fund doesn't need to be in the millions. However, it should be enough to give you some peace of mind. It should save you from begging your friends or family members for help if any tragedy befalls you.

So, how can one go about setting a savings fund?

It's quite simple, actually. Take a look at your lifestyle and find out your weak areas. For example, you have a thing for designer handbags and always look for a good bargain. It's time you set aside your handbag shopping hobby aside and save the amount for the future.

Try to save at least six months' worth of expenses to have ample time to get back up on your feet.

Buying a House Should Always Be An Option

"The biggest adventure you can ever take is to live the life of your dreams."

There's nothing wrong with dreaming big! Take a look at any retired media personality, and you will see they have lavish homes in different cities. Oprah herself has multiple houses in Washington, California, Hawaii, and Colorado. She has spent around $140 million on real estate. This portfolio does not include the properties she previously owned in Illinois, Georgia, and Florida.

One of the best things about real estate is that its value does not plummet. This quality makes it a lucrative investment. After building equity, you can draw on it and borrow money as many times as you want.

Often people say that don't tire yourself by working too much or you will miss life. Oprah believes in the opposite.

Oprah started her career at a young age. Although she was not paid for her college speeches, she put in the time and effort to hone her skills. Later on, she worked seven days a week.

She worked hard day and night. Today, life has rewarded her with comforts that people envy.

A Single Goal Is What Unites Us

"Surround yourself only with people who are going to take you higher."

Every person in life has a single goal: to become successful. However, not everyone can achieve them. To reach our full potential, we put our skills to the test. Our quest to be successful should not lead us to join the rat race but look at the status quo.

There's nothing wrong with climbing the social ladder. The climb will be hard but do not push someone aside to get what you want.

Education Is Vital for Progress

"Create the highest grandest vision for your life. Then let every step move you in that direction."

Oprah has stated many times that her father's love and enthusiasm for learning turned her life around. Your vision and attitude change the way you think about things.

You will find that your perspective is different from others. However, as long as it is right, you don't need to worry about doing the wrong thing.

Oprah learned this lesson the hard way, which she has described in an article in the O Magazine. She helped several low-income families in Chicago by moving them into new homes. Her idea was to show people how they can build successful lives. However, the experience proved to be overwhelming.

At the time, Oprah hadn't considered that these people juggle multiple lives. They go to work, have to be there on time, make sure their children go to school, put food on the table, etc. So, she failed but learned a valuable less: You can't just give people what they want. For your offering to be valuable, you first need to transform the way people see things. Once you change their mindset, you will improve their life.

Oprah's Debt Diet Process

More than a decade ago, Oprah came up with a Debt Diet Process that helped people manage their debt in 8 steps. To this day, her fans still follow her advice.

The process allowed people to take control of their debt, including loan debt like student loans, mortgages, unpaid bills, and credit card debt.

Following are eight steps that will help you control and eliminate your debt:

The Debt Diet Process is divided into two phases. Phase 1 helps you tackle short-term goals, which include the small things. In Phase 2, you look at your long-term goals and come up with a strategy to keep your debt in check for more savings.

Phase 1 – Short-Term Goals

Step #1

Find Out the Amount of Debt You Have

You mostly go into debt due to unpaid bills and delayed credit card payments. So, the first thing you need to do is get a copy of your credit report. This report will give you an idea of how much you need to pay.

Sometimes, it can be a little difficult to find out how much debt you are under. Hence, you should track your bills and keep an eye on the purchases you make with your credit card. The free credit report you are entitled to every year will all you to prioritize your purchases.

For example, if you are considering buying something costly, review your monthly expenses.

- First, support your family and yourself.
- Second, pay back your loans. (Student loans, mortgages, credit card payments, etc.)
- Third, increase your savings.
- Fourth, mark your luxury expenses, which you can afford with the money you have left after the priorities.

Step #2

Track Your Spending – Follow the Latte Factor®

People have a big misconception about building their wealth. They think it's all about income. In reality, your spending habits determine how much you save.

Most people don't pay attention to how much they spend. We are not talking about large purchases but the small ones they make daily.

For example, you will probably think twice before purchasing an iPhone or expensive gadget but not before getting a coffee from the cart parked on your street.

This approach is called the Latte Factor®, a term that financial author David Bach coined. According to him, if you save the money you spend on daily lattes, you can build up a small fortune and do it faster.

When you hear this idea for the first time, it does not hold much merit. However, if you give it some thought, you will realize that you always achieve your goals by starting small.

This concept tells you to save $10 every day and put it towards resolving your debt rather than spending it on a bagel and fancy coffee.

So, stop buying a soda and sandwich from the vending machine in your office. Track your purchases and cut back wherever you can.

Step #3

Learn the Credit Card Game

High interest rates, annual and late fees, and penalties are just some of the pitfalls of a credit card. You might get bamboozled with the minimum payments, but when not made on time, they quickly add up and push you into debt for longer.

So, what can you do to become a master in this game?

First of all, make more than your minimum payment. This way, your debt will be small at the end of the month. By making payments on time, you can build a positive credit history.

When you make payments on time, you can contact your bank and ask them if they can lower the interest rate. Don't forget to do your homework before making the call. If the agent does not agree, you can tell them how their competitors offer lower rates.

If you are up to date with your payments and are planning to get a new credit card, keep these four things in mind: Late fees, interest rates, teaser offers, and annual fees. These points will allow you to compare offers and make an informed decision.

Having multiple credit cards is a huge responsibility. You need to figure out which credit card to pay off first. In theory, it always makes sense to pay off the bigger ones first and put a small amount towards the smaller ones.

Step #4

Stop Spending Freely

Your spending habit is the first thing you need to control when it comes to savings. The best way to do this is to not carry your debit or credit card with you when running small errands. As mentioned earlier, try to make all your payments on time when using your credit card.

This tip sounds very simple in theory, but following it can be a little difficult. Live by the mantra, *"I won't buy things I can't afford."*

Phase 2 – Long-Term Goals

Step #5

Create a Spending Plan

Have you ever tracked how much you spend in a day or a month? If you wonder where all the money went, it's time to create a budget.

Your budget should include housing expenses and costs, transportation, and other expenses. Create a separate budget for debts so that you can track how much is being put and where.

Step #6

Grow Your Income

Ask anyone how you can increase your income, and they will tell you to start a side hustle. Juggling two jobs can be quite difficult. Not only will you find yourself trapped in work, but you won't be able to carve out some "me" time.

Since this step falls under *Long-Term Goals*, you need to go big. Again, start small by cutting back on your weekend outings and takeout.

When going big, consider your housing expenses. If they are too high, consider relocating. If possible, take public transport to work and save on fuel.

If you have valuable items you are not emotionally attached to, get them appraised and sell them. Put the money in a CD saving account.

This weekend, brainstorm ideas on what more you can do to make money. Note down your skills, and then find out how you can use them to earn online.

Step #7

Raise Your Credit Score

Lower your debt.

Three simple words, right? However, it can be a huge challenge to follow them.

First, find out what debts are secured (Debts backed by collateral) and unsecured. For example, you applied for a payday loan that asked for collateral. You decided to use your car as a backup. Unfortunately, you lost your job and couldn't make the last six monthly payments. As a result, the lender possessed your car.

For this reason, you need to satisfy your debts in the following order:

- Secured Debts
- Unsecured debts (Credit cards)
- Debts that might be automatically paid as soon as your paycheck arrives
- Service, such as insurance that is important for your wellbeing
- Debts to friends and family

By lowering your debt, you will increase your credit score. A higher credit score will help your secure a loan with low interest rates in the future.

Step #8

Think Twice Before Spending

When you earn more and have multiple credit cards, it can be a little difficult to curb your spending. However, spending out of your limit at the moment can leave you empty-handed in the future.

Here's an example to help you understand the gravity of this situation:

Mary works a 9 to 5 job as a video editor. On average, a video editor makes $4,375/month. A top earner's monthly pay in this field is $8,291/month. Mary earns a little more than

$5,000/month. As a single mother, she earns quite well and can send her two kids to a good school.

The problem is that Mary is a shopaholic. She doesn't hoard things, but she does own an impressive collection of designer shoes and purses. As the next month rolls around, her boss tells her that they will be taking on a new project that will require overtime, and they will pay her handsomely.

She takes the opportunity, and that month, she gets a paycheck of $15,000. Ecstatic, she decides to treat herself and her children. She spends almost the entire amount on getting her kids iPads and the rest on clothes and jewelry. As you can guess, she puts nothing aside for savings.

Two months later, she gets into an accident. She comes out without a scratch, but her kids get several injuries. With no money saved for emergencies, Mary asks her colleagues for a loan. Some deny her request outright, while others could only give her a few hundred dollars.

Ultimately, she had to take out a loan and sell some of her belongings to make ends meet.

Figuring out how much you spend and how to change your lifestyle is a problem that requires professional help.

Oprah's self-assessment is that you should consult a therapist or discuss the problem with family members and friends.

Once you have completed the 8th step, work on your *after-debt* plan:

Make a Plan

There's a reason why you went into debt. Once you are free of it, you should come up with a plan to never end up in that place again.

Think back on the reasons why you curbed your spending. Use that as a basis for developing the plan. Create a to-do list to manage your money.

Write down your short-term and long-term goals. Some of them could be:

- Do not spend on non-essential items
- Use the "Envelope System" to divide your money for errands and leisure time
- Avoid temptations by telling yourself you have other, more important responsibilities

Budget

Just because you are debt-free does not mean that you will never spend again. There will come a time when the temptation will prove to be too much, and you will splurge.

Plan for such an occasion in advance. For example, you could save a dollar here or there for your leisure expenses. However, you need to set a budget for this splurge, so you don't go out of range.

Set Up Your Savings Account

Having a savings account is a must! You should always save at least 15% to 25% of your paycheck. One of the best things about opening a savings account is that it allows you to earn interest on your money. You just need to let it sit untouched for a certain period; you will get a small percentage of your savings.

Invest

There are multiple ways to invest your savings. However, you need to take this step carefully to ensure you don't put your money in the wrong place.

Better consult a financial advisor to know about your options. If you work a 9-to-5 job, get a 401k. A 401k will help you create your retirement savings. Remember that the money you put forward for the 401k will remain in the account until you are 60 years old. If you withdraw the money early, you will incur a penalty.

Based on this information, you can say that Oprah's Debt Diet process is a great way to save money and keep track of your debt.

Changing your spending habits according to the lifestyle you lead can be a little difficult. Hence, you first need to turn around your life and figure out how big of a role money plays in your life.

Prioritize your needs and then think long and hard about your wants. Your needs include the necessities in your life, such as paying bills, grocery shopping, rent, and insurance. As for wants, they are mostly luxuries that help you lead a comfortable life. So, differentiate between your needs and wants to get started, and then follow the steps to get your life back on track.

A Timeline of Oprah Winfrey's Life

<table>
<tr><td align="center">Oprah Winfrey – The Queen of All Media</td></tr>
<tr><td align="center">A Timeline of Oprah's Life and Struggles</td></tr>
<tr><td>January 29, 1954

Oprah Winfrey Gail is born in Kosciusko, Mississippi.</td></tr>
<tr><td>1816 – Mother Left

Oprah's mother, Vernita Lee, leaves her with her grandmother Hattie Mae Lee and goes up north searching for a job and home.</td></tr>
<tr><td>1956 – Oprah's Learning Begins

Oprah's grandmother teaches her how to read and write.</td></tr>
<tr><td>1957 – Oprah Joins Church

Oprah starts reciting Bible verses in front of the church crowd and develops a passion for public speaking.</td></tr>
<tr><td>1959 – Her Official Learning Begins

Oprah attends kindergarten and skips 1st grade because she is a talented child. Her father takes her to libraries so she can read books.</td></tr>
<tr><td>1960 to 1961 – Pursues Her Passion for Speaking</td></tr>
</table>

Starts speaking in school gatherings.

Gets paid $500 to speak in front of a live audience.

1962 – Goes Back to Her Mother

Her father moves her back to live with her mother.

1963 – Her Sexual Abuse Begins

She is raped by her 19-year-old cousin, uncle, and a family friend.

1967 – Runs Away from Home

After enduring four years of sexual abuse, Oprah ran away from home. However, she is caught by the authorities and starts living with her father again.

1967 – Finds Out She Is Pregnant

While caring for her father, Oprah found out she was pregnant. Sadly, her baby doesn't survive the birth, and her father helps her overcome the loss.

1970 – Gets Full Scholarship to a University and Becomes a News Anchor at a Radio Station

After leaving her past behind, Oprah manages to win a full ride to Tennessee State University. Because of her passion for speaking, she gets a position as a news anchor at a radio station.

1972 – Wins Miss Black Tennessee

Oprah enters beauty pageants and wins the title of Miss Black Tennessee.

1973 – Becomes a News Anchor

Oprah joins as a news anchor and co-host on WJZ alongside her newscast Jerry Turner.

1978 – Becomes Co-Host on the Talk Show "People Are Talking."

When Oprah can't handle the tough job of being a news anchor and asking sensitive questions, the network demotes her to a local talk show called "People Are Talking."

1986 – Gets Hired by ABC

Oprah strikes gold with "People Are Talking" as it gains worldwide attention. ABC hires her to bring up the ratings of their failing show.

1986 – The Talk Show Is Renamed

Oprah's presence on ABC's talk show increases its ratings immediately. The channel executives are so happy that they decide to rename the show to The Oprah Winfrey Show.

1897 – Oprah's Success Begins

Once she had garnered the world's attention through her talk show, she started getting multiple offers in the media industry. She partnered with multiple companies, opened a few of her own, and received the Medal of Freedom from Barack Obama and many more accolades thanks to her words and actions.

Conclusion

Now everyone gets the chance or opportunities to succeed in life. Sometimes, you have to search for them or create them on your own to fulfill your dream.

Oprah Winfrey was and is more than a talk show host. She is best known for putting people in a comfortable position so they can open up to her. However, she has many more talents.

As an award-winning actress, media mogul, producer, and philanthropist, she has proved to the world that if you put your mind to it, you can do it all.

The comforts Oprah enjoys today did not come easily to her. She overcame many obstacles, two of the biggest being sexually abused at a younger age and being sidelines for positions because of her race and soft heart.

However, she didn't let her childhood and early career failures come in between her goals. Despite the challenges she faced, Oprah persevered.

Nowadays, Oprah is invested in her book club and the weekly newsletter *Oprah Insider*. Every week, she sets an intention to reflect on topics such as forgiveness, letting go, being the person you were meant to be, and more.

One of her most impactful themes was *being open to the lessons life teaches us*. We all go through numerous experiences that keep repeating in our lives. Sometimes, these experiences help you grow and allow you to face the real you in the mirror.

We all know the earth is round. Oprah sees the world as a classroom with the earth as the school. As the earth orbits, new things come to light now and then. So, in a way, the lessons never stop.

You might say "no" to something at the moment, but the situation will present itself differently. There's one thing you should always remind yourself of when you are stuck in a situation: Life always works out in the end.

Oprah didn't give up when she was demoted. She didn't leave the talk show when she thought it would destroy her career. She didn't back down from interviewing people when the world was against them. It all comes down to your willpower and how much you are willing to sacrifice for your passion.

Once you get on board with what's in front of you, your life changes on a certain level. You feel this vibration go through you, turning you into a new person. So, absorb those changes and hope for the best because your story is never over until you say so.

Disclaimer